Introduction

The he windows in King's College Chapel are one of the glories of the European Renaissance and give an insight into the theological thinking and daily life of the late Middle Ages.

There are four scenes in each window. These depict incidents from the life of Jesus, legends of Mary his mother, stories of the apostles and Old Testament stories. In most, the upper and lower scenes on each side are linked; the lower is from the New Testament, and above is a parallel scene from the Old Testament. Linking Bible stories in this way is called 'typology' and is based on the belief that God is the same 'yesterday, today and for ever'. So studying a previous, similar incident will bring a deeper understanding of the ways of God. Occasionally an opposite or 'antitype' is used. This way of thinking goes back to the Bible itself and was a favourite study in the early Church and throughout the Middle Ages. It fell into disfavour, but in recent years some have returned to it, considering it a truly Biblical way of bringing out the deeper meaning of a story.

The plan of the windows was drawn up by Richard Fox, Bishop of Winchester, one of Henry VII's statesmen. Mainly, he used a standard scheme, similar to the thirteenth-century book *Biblia Pauperum*. But Bishop Fox was committed to the New Learning and a friend of the scholars Colet and Erasmus. Theologians of the New Learning explored questions about the authority of the early Church, studying the Acts of the Apostles and the letters of Paul. Therefore, unusually for such schemes, scenes from the Acts of the Apostles are to be found in windows 21, 22 and 23.

King's College was founded by King Henry VI in 1441. Building ceased during the Civil War but was restarted by Henry VII. He died in 1509, leaving money to complete the building. The magnificent fan vaulting of the roof belongs to the last period of construction and was completed in three years under the supervision of the Master Mason, John Wastell. The building was finished in 1515, and work on the windows started immediately with money left by Henry VII. At various periods during his reign, his son, Henry VIII, gave money for more of the windows, but the West Window remained plain glass on his death. The scheme was only completed in the nineteenth century.

The Chapel was built as a place of worship for the scholars and students of King's College, and that remains its principal function. Members of the public often attend the college services because of the high standard of music reached by the Chapel Choir. The Chapel is best known for the Christmas Eve service of Nine Lessons and Carols, broadcast live by the BBC. To many, listening to that service is an integral part of Christmas celebrations and has made the Chapel a place of interest.

This booklet aims to guide you round the windows and touch on the deep theological message they convey. If you are short of time, it would be better to look at a few windows thoroughly rather than hurry past many.

There are four Messengers in the central lights of each of the side windows (see Chapel plan opposite). These show angels, prophets and biblical writers holding scrolls. Some designs appear more than once, often in different colours. The scrolls have biblical texts referring to the four scenes in the window. Above is the fourth Messenger (M4) from Window 17.

Window I

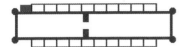

A. Mary's parents at the Golden Gate
Early Christian legend

B. Joachim's offering is rejected
Early Christian legend

C. The birth of Mary
Early Christian legend

D. An angel appears to Joachim
Early Christian legend

The four scenes in this window tell the legend of the miraculous birth of Mary, the mother of Jesus. This legend stresses that Mary was set apart from birth and so emphasises her importance in God's plan of salvation for the world. Unusually, it is best to take the scenes in the order B, D, A, C, the way the story is told.

B. The main figure is Joachim, leaving the Temple because his offering has been rejected. His wife, Anna, is behind him. The High Priest, Reuben, wearing a crown, thrusts the offering away because the couple are childless. The Temple is shown as an elaborate Renaissance-style cathedral with, above the altar, a statue of Moses carrying the stone tablets of the Law.

D. After his rejection, Joachim retired to the countryside. The scene shows a green winged angel appearing to Joachim, who is dressed as a wealthy landowner. His steward stands behind him, and around are the sheep, shepherds (one playing bagpipes) and dogs. The angel tells Joachim to return to the Temple. The scene is more sixteenth-century Norfolk than first-century Palestine because the glaziers painted what they knew.

A. Joachim meets his wife at the Golden Gate of the Temple. They kiss, and Mary is conceived. The tree on the left refers to the Tree of Jesse. Jesse was David's father, and Isaiah II:I–2 refers to a Branch growing out of the stem of Jesse, which was seen as a reference to Jesus. Joachim, Anna and Mary's husband, Joseph, were all believed to be descendants of King David.

C. Below, Anna and her maid attend to the baby. Above, Anna sits up ready

to receive her friends. This legend of the birth of Mary dates from the second century, but English people of the early sixteenth century would know it from *The Golden Legend*, one of the first books printed in England by Caxton.

All Christians accept Mary's part in God's plan of Salvation but understand it differently. Protestants see her as part of humanity, not separate; Eastern Orthodox Christians give her the title 'Panagia' (All-holy) and Roman Catholics celebrate the Doctrine of the Immaculate Conception on 8 December.

Window 2

A. Dedication of Mary
Early Christian legend
B. Dedication of the Golden Table
Classical legend

C. Marriage of Mary and Joseph
Early Christian legend
D. Marriage of Sarah and Tobias
Tobit 7:13–14

Scenes A and C continue the legend of Mary, with 'types' above. This window is early, and the small figures, similar to those in a mediaeval manuscript, are unique to it.

A. Mary, aged seven, is dedicated to God by her parents in the Temple. The High Priest stands ready to receive her. This legend is an amalgamation of the Jewish practice of dedicating first-born boys (never girls) and the Roman Vestal Virgins.

B. Two fishermen dedicate a Golden Table, which has appeared miraculously in their nets, to the sun god Apollo. Solon of Athens looks on as they follow his advice. Mediaeval scholars saw this legend as a 'type' of the dedication of Mary by her parents.

C. The hands of Mary and Joseph are joined in marriage by the Bishop. Mary's hair is loose round her shoulders, showing she is a virgin. Joseph holds the staff which, when it sprouted, indicated he was the man chosen to be Mary's husband. Rejected suitors walk away.

D. The main figures are Sarah, Tobias and Sarah's father. Tobias is being encouraged by the young man, who is really the angel Raphael. Sarah's long flowing hair indicates her virginity, the cause of Tobias' reluctance. Seven previous husbands had been killed before they could consummate the marriage!

The sparse references to Mary, Mother of Jesus, in the New Testament were felt to be inadequate by later Christians, so legends of her early life developed. Joseph is mentioned even less, but his legacy is the frequency with which Jesus compared the love of God to that of a father.

Window 3 *(left scenes)*

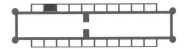

A. The announcement to Mary
St Luke 1:26–38
B. The temptation of Eve
Genesis 3:1–6

The contrast in the left-hand scenes is between the obedience of Mary and the disobedience of Eve. Another contrast is in the ways of acquiring wisdom. Mary studies, but Eve takes what she has been told to leave alone.

A. The archangel Gabriel, dressed as the ambassador of a mediaeval king, greets Mary, who looks up from her book. Her flowing hair shows her virginity, and the lilies are symbols of purity especially associated with the Annunciation. Mary accepts her role as mother of the saviour, so a shaft of light strikes down, and above her

DETAIL

hovers a dove, surrounded by rays of glory, symbolising of the Holy Spirit of God. The lettering on the cornice reads ECCE ANCILLA DOMINA ('behold the handmaid of the Lord'), the Latin translation of Mary's reply to Gabriel. Mary's open book has an illuminated initial like sixteenth-century Bibles. The books and the lamp, the Psalmist's symbol of wisdom, are reminders of the wisdom that comes from reverent study of the Scriptures.

B. Adam and Eve's expulsion from the Garden of Eden is symbolic of the way all humanity is separated from God. The profundity of this story is better understood if it is remembered that Adam and Eve are 'Everyman' and 'Everywoman'. On the left, Eve listens to the Serpent and accepts the fruit of the tree. The Serpent leans over, encouraging her to eat it. The fruit is from the Tree of Knowledge of Good and Evil, which they had been commanded to leave alone. In Latin, *malum* (apple) and *malus* (evil) are similar, so an apple has widely been assumed, though the name is not in Genesis. As usual in mediaeval paintings, the serpent is half human and, not surprising in a chapel built for celibate young men, clearly female. In the background is the gate through which Adam and Eve are expelled.

The contrast is between Eve's disobedience and Mary's obedience. As the mediaeval pun said, 'Eve' was turned to 'Ave' (Hail – Gabriel's first word, repeated in popular devotion). In the Christian calendar 25 March, or Lady Day, is celebrated as the Feast of the Annunciation (announcement to Mary).

Window 3 *(right scenes)*

C. The birth of Jesus
St Luke 2:6–17
D. The burning bush
Exodus 3:1–6

In these lights the birth of Jesus is paired with a very important Old Testament event, the appearance of God to Moses in the burning bush. In both, God begins the process of salvation, showing his loving care for his people.

C. Mary kneels before the baby Jesus, who is lying in a manger surrounded by angels. Joseph is behind Mary, shielding a candle. By the manger stand the animals and two shepherds, one playing bagpipes. Two more shepherds are just arriving. Above the main scene is a small picture of the shepherds listening to the angel and, just below the window transom is the sun, a reminder that Jesus is given the Old Testament title 'Son Of Righteousness'. This scene is familiar from Christmas cards and crib scenes, though the details are more Tudor England than first-century Palestine.

D. When God appeared to Moses in the burning bush, he commanded him to go to Egypt to set the Israelites free. Moses is hastily removing his shoes as he realises the holiness of the place. God is shown in human form, surrounded by an aureole, a field of radiance symbolising divinity. On his knee is an orb, indicating his sovereignty over the world. His hand is stretched out in command to Moses. Both these scenes are technically 'theophanies' – occasions when God appears to human beings.

The birth of Jesus has been celebrated on 25 December since the fourth century. It is not known when Jesus was born, but everyone had a holiday for the pagan sun festival, so Christians celebrated the birth of the 'Sun of Righteousness'.

Window 4

A. The circumcision of Jesus
St Luke 2:21

B. The circumcision of Isaac
Genesis 21:3–4

C. Foreign wise men bring gifts
St Matthew 2:1–11

D. A foreign queen brings gifts
1 Kings 10:1–10

This window continues the story of the birth of Jesus, moving from one Gospel to another. Luke, the Gentile Gospel writer, recorded that Jesus' parents obeyed Jewish laws and customs. Matthew, the Jewish Evangelist, recorded the visit of the Gentile wise men. (Mark and John do not have anything on Jesus' birth.)

A. Jesus was born a Jew, so, eight days after being born, he was circumcised and named. In the window, the baby lies on a cushion, while the celebrant, on the right, is shown holding a knife in his hand and wearing glasses, which had not been invented in the first century. Behind stand Mary and Joseph and two women holding candles similar to those used at an early sixteenth-century baptism. In both ceremonies the baby received a name and was acknowledged as having a separate very special identity. 'Jesus' is the Greek form of the Hebrew name 'Joshua' and means 'God saves'.

B. The upper scene is of the circumcision of Isaac, and the main figures are shown the opposite way round from those in the picture below. Abraham, Isaac's father, who is performing the ceremony, was given the title 'Friend of God', and circumcision was a sign of that relationship with God. These scenes stress that the spiritual care of a baby is as important as the physical care and an important responsibility of parenthood.

C. On the left, the three wise men bow and present their gifts to Jesus, who is sitting on his mother's lap. Joseph stands behind Mary with an ox and a donkey, indicating they are still in the stable. The wise man on the left has negroid features,

following the tradition that the three were an African, an Asian and a European. Above the main scene are two small pictures of earlier stages of the story. In the middle the three are consulting their astrology books, and above they ride in chariots, following the star. The Gospel implies that the wise men were Gentiles (non-Jews) but does not say how many there were. Three are assumed as there are three gifts: gold representing kingship, frankincense for divinity and myrrh for suffering and death.

D. King Solomon had a reputation for great wisdom, so the Queen of Sheba, a distant and exotic land, came to see for herself. The window shows the Queen offering a gold vessel to Solomon, who is seated on an elaborate throne. Everyone is dressed in magnificent robes, similar to those of the Tudor court. The glazier has made Solomon look like Henry VIII, following the lead of the

court painter, Hans Holbein. At the time the window was painted, 1535, the break with Rome had taken place, and it was important to stress that the King and the Church of England were dependent for faith on God alone and not Rome. Other representations of Solomon in the chapel (windows 12 and 25) were made earlier and do not use this idea. It is possible that the Queen, who is wearing the very fashionable French hood, is a representation of Katherine Howard, Henry's Queen at the time the window was painted, but no portrait of her has survived.

In the Christian calendar, the circumcision and naming of Jesus is celebrated on 1 January and the arrival of the wise men on 6 January, Epiphany. Epiphany means manifestation (revelation or showing). The festival celebrates the revelation to the Gentiles, represented by the wise men.

Window 5 *(left scenes)*

A. The dedication of Jesus
St Luke 2:22–38
B. The dedication of the first-born
Exodus 13:2

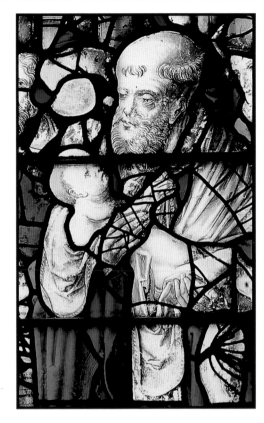

These lights continue the story of the birth of Jesus and complete the account of his family's fulfilment of the Law with the dedication of Jesus and the purification of his mother. To many pious Jews the dedication of the first-born symbolised their unique calling among the nations. Christians see Jesus as fulfilling earlier prophecies in his lifelong dedication.

A. Mary and Joseph, who is carrying a basket of doves, are on the left. On the right, Simeon is holding the baby. Above Simeon, an old woman wearing an old-fashioned red steeple hat is coming to join them. As Mary's first-born was a boy, the Jewish Law required that he was dedicated to God. When Mary and Joseph arrived in the Temple in Jerusalem for the ceremony they were met by an old holy man, Simeon, who recognised Jesus as the Saviour. Anna, the old woman in the red hat, was another who recognised him and told everyone. In Luke's Gospel, Simeon, in his joy, speaks in poetry and the words form the canticle *Nunc Dimittis*, 'Lord, now lettest thou thy servant depart in peace', which became part of evening worship in the monasteries and from there into Evensong in Anglican churches. The doves that Joseph is carrying belong to the ceremony marking the purification of the woman which took place 40 days after the birth of a boy. The doves were the poor man's concessionary sacrifice. There seems to be some confusion between the two ceremonies, possibly going back to Luke himself.

B. The scene also shows the dedication by a woman of her first-born, who is a boy. This ceremony goes back to the Exodus, when the tenth plague spared the first-born of the Israelites when it swept through Egypt.

The Presentation of Christ in the Temple is celebrated on 2 February, often called Candlemas. As it is 40 days after 25 December it is also the feast of the purification of the Virgin Mary. In the Middle Ages the Cistercian Monasteries had a special reverence for Mary and imported snowdrops to decorate the altars at Candlemas.

Window 5 *(right scenes)*

C. The flight into Egypt
St Matthew 2:14
D. Jacob and Esau
Genesis 27:1–28:5

DETAIL

These scenes give an assurance of God's protection in time of trouble, especially for those who have to flee for their lives. Joseph takes his family to Egypt for safety, and Jacob flees from his brother, whom he has cheated. Jacob's story is a reminder that God's grace is not earned by merit but is given freely.

C. Joseph, wearing a broad-brimmed traveller's hat, leads the donkey down a stony path by a stream. King Herod had learned enough from the wise men to fear a rival and planned to kill him. Joseph, warned by a dream, escaped to Egypt. Four early legends about the journey are illustrated here. The stream had bubbled up when the family ran out of water. In the middle distance, two men carry bundles to help the fugitives, and in the centre, an image falls from a pink pillar as Jesus passes. In the background, soldiers in a chariot stop by a cornfield. Convinced by the reapers that the fugitives had passed when the corn was sown, the soldiers turn back, not realising that the corn had sprung up and ripened in a day.

D. The main scene shows Esau about to ask his blind father, Isaac, for the blessing of the first-born. He then discovers that his brother Jacob has tricked his father. When Esau discovers that he has been tricked out of his inheritance he is so angry that Jacob has to flee for his life. While the primary link between these two scenes is the need to flee, their connection is deeper – in both cases the flight was necessary because of greed for power. Herod could not tolerate the thought of a rival, even an infant. Jacob's trickery and Esau's anger show how much power mattered to them both – they were even prepared to destroy their family unit in its pursuit.

In the upper scene Esau is carrying a longbow because he has come in from hunting, but in mediaeval England a bow was a military weapon – a means of killing others. It represents the lengths to which hunger for power can lead an individual or a nation. Both scenes remind the viewer that force, even overwhelming military might, cannot prevail against God.

C

Window 6 *(left scenes)*

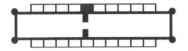

A. The fall of the idols
Early Christian legend
B. The Golden Calf
Exodus 32:1–19

DETAIL

The lower scene illustrates an old legend that is linked with the Old Testament story of the Golden Calf. The place of physical representations of God in worship was a very live issue at the time the window was painted.

A. The legend said that the temple idols fell when the Holy Family arrived in the Egyptian city, and the Governor was so awestruck that he worshipped the Holy Child. The organ loft obscures much of this scene, but two idols can be seen falling from their pillars. Below is the Governor and Mary carrying the Holy Child. This legend comes from the eighth-century 'Gospel of the Pseudo-Matthew'. At the time the window was made, it was difficult for people to distinguish between legend and Bible story because Bibles were often produced in sections and the legends were also in short books. Popular books like *The Golden Legend*, one of the first books printed by Caxton, combined the two.

B. The Old Testament scene shows the Golden Calf, on top of a tall red pillar, being worshipped by the Israelites. They had made the calf while Moses was up Mount Sinai receiving the Ten Commandments from God. On the left Moses has just arrived back and discovered what has happened. The tablets of the Commandments lie broken at his feet. The small horns on his head are usual in representations of Moses on Mount Sinai. When Jerome translated the Bible into Latin (known as the Vulgate and used throughout the Middle Ages) he mistook *qeren* (horn) for *qaran* (shine). Thus, when describing Moses coming from the presence of God, Jerome wrote 'horns had sprouted on his head' instead of 'the skin of his face shone'. This error in translation occurred because Hebrew was originally written in consonants only.

B

Christians have often used images (icons, pictures and statues) but there has always been a tension between the benefits and perceived risks of religious imagery. It can aid concentration but also risk compromising belief in the spiritual nature of God as emphasised in the Ten Commandments.

Window 6 *(right scenes)*

C. Killing the children
St Matthew 2:16–18
D. Killing the royal children
2 Kings 11:1–2

In the lower scene, a tragic footnote to the visit of the wise men concludes the account of the birth of Jesus. The upper scene shows an equally brutal but ultimately unsuccessful attempt to eliminate rivals. Although these scenes are gruesome, the theme of the window is reassurance – these brutal actions did not defeat the will of God.

C. When the wise men first arrived in Palestine, they went to Jerusalem, expecting to find the new-born king in the palace. This alerted King Herod to the possibility of a rival. Herod decided to kill all the children under two in Bethlehem, to eliminate his possible rival. As previous windows have shown, Jesus and his family escaped to Egypt. The scene in this window shows a woman, half turned away, attempting to protect her child from a soldier, while, behind her, another soldier is about to kill a child with a knife. The slaughter is overseen by an officer on horseback, and near him is a group of soldiers with a banner. In the middle distance is a village with a huddle of frightened people. In his last years, Herod the Great became increasingly suspicious and brutal, even executing his own son. There is no non-Biblical record of this incident, but it fits a known pattern.

D. The Old Testament scene is from a story in the book of Kings. When Queen Athaliah's son died, she would have lost the power and influence that she enjoyed as the Queen Mother, in Judah a position second only to that of the king. So she killed the male members of the Royal Family and seized the throne for herself. One of her grandsons was hidden by his aunt, Jehosheba.

Six years later a coup overthrew Athaliah. The window shows Athaliah, in red, holding a sceptre, supervising the slaughter of the children by a number of soldiers, one wearing a Viking-like winged helmet. Above stands Jehosheba, holding the baby prince, in full view of the rampaging soldiers. This defiant stance does not fit the Bible story, which describes how Jehosheba smuggled the child out of the palace and hid him in the temple complex. If the window was not obscured by the organ loft, it would be seen that

Jehosheba, with the prince in her arms, balances Mary, with the child Jesus in her arms, depicted in the bottom left-hand scene.

The elimination of rivals was common in sixteenth-century Europe. The Tudor dynasty's claim to the throne was weak, so its rivals were executed. This window shows that kings may kill, but God's purpose will triumph. In the Christian calendar, the children of Bethlehem, the Holy Innocents, are remembered on 28 December.

Window 7 *(left scenes)*

A. The baptism of Jesus
St Matthew 3:13–17
B. The healing of Naaman
2 Kings 5:1–14

All the Gospels describe John the Baptist preaching in the wilderness and calling people to repent and be baptised in the Jordan. Jesus was one of those who responded, and his baptism is the moment of self dedication for his ministry.

A. This scene shows Jesus coming out of the River Jordan after his baptism while John the Baptist sits on the bank, his hand raised to sprinkle water over him. The attendant angels hold Jesus' clothes. Just below the transom, God the Father is shown sending his Holy Spirit, symbolised by the dove hovering over Jesus. The importance of the moment is indicated by the rays of glory surrounding the dove and by the halo over the head of Jesus, which the glaziers only used when depicting very sacred occasions. The stag in the background is an Old Testament symbol of religious aspiration.

B. The main figure is Naaman, who was told by the prophet Elisha to bathe seven times in the River Jordan if he wished to be healed. In spite of his scepticism, Naaman was persuaded to do this by his servants. One servant is holding his clothes, and others wait in the background. All are dressed as gallants in attendance on a sixteenth-century nobleman.

These stories were linked in *Speculum Humanae Salvationis* ('Mirror of Man's Salvation'), a fourteenth-century devotional book, partly because they involved bathing in the Jordan; but salvation also includes a wide range of meanings, including safety, healing (as with Naaman), a new start in the relationship with God (the aim of the baptism of John) and putting that relationship on a completely new basis, which the ministry of Jesus brings.

Window 7 *(right scenes)*

C. The temptation of Jesus
St Matthew 4:1–11
D. Jacob tempts Esau
Genesis 25:29–33

During the period in the wilderness, immediately after his baptism, Jesus was tempted, and one temptation involved food. In the Old Testament story, Esau was also tempted with food, but he gave in and traded his birthright for immediate gratification. Jesus, in contrast, rejected the temptation.

C. The main figures are Jesus, on the left, dressed in royal purple, and Satan, dressed as a friar and holding an armfull of stones. A popular name for the devil was 'Old Hornie', so he is shown as an old man with horns pushing up his friar's cowl. Friars claimed to serve God and the poor in the towns of mediaeval Europe, but many had a bad reputation for greed and exploitation by the time the window was painted. The whole story of Jesus being tempted in the wilderness is illustrated: the stones that are to be turned to bread; the turrets and pinnacles from which Jesus was tempted to leap (on the right, above the main scene); and the devil pointing to the kingdoms of the world (above, on the left). These temptations were alternative ways that Jesus might have carried out his ministry: by using his powers to make life more comfortable for himself and others; by proving his credentials; and by fulfilling the popular expectation of a warrior king like David. His rejection of these meant the alternative – the Way of the Cross. The scenery is an English not Palestinian wilderness, with dense woodland, a bear, hares, a hedgehog, flowers, butterflies and fungi.

D. The main figures are Jacob, sitting at a table, and Esau, standing with his hand out. Esau is coming in from the hunt, carrying a bow in his hand, his quiver still on and his bright red hat

pushed onto his back. His exhausted dog droops by his feet, and an attendant follows him in. A servant stands behind the table with a pan holding the lentil broth, while Jacob has a deep plate and a spoon in front of him on the table. Behind the door, their mother, Rebekah, listens as her favourite gains advantage over his brother. Esau's hunger gives Jacob his opportunity, and Esau trades his birthright for food. Another part of the story of the rivalry between these twin brothers is told in Window 5, scene D.

When Jesus rejected the first temptation, he quoted from the Old Testament, 'Man cannot live by bread alone: he lives on every word that God utters'. In our materialistic age, it is easy to forget that material prosperity, although important, is ultimately not the thing that brings true happiness. In the Christian calendar, Jesus' period in the wilderness is remembered during Lent, the 40 days leading up to the Holy Week before Easter.

Window 8

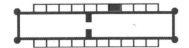

A. The raising of Lazarus
St John 11:17–44
B. Elisha raises the Shunamite boy
2 Kings 4:18–37

C. Jesus enters Jerusalem
St John 12:12–15
D. David enters Jerusalem
1 Samuel 17:54 and 18:5–6

The New Testament scenes come from the end of Jesus' public ministry and ask the question, what did Jesus come to save people from? The entry into Jerusalem made it clear he did not come to save them from the Romans. As is usual in the Chapel, Jesus is shown wearing purple, symbolising royal or imperial status. White, the colour of holiness, was preferred by other painters, particularly the Victorians.

A. Jesus is shown with his hand raised in command to Lazarus, rising from his tomb. The grave wrappings fall off, while discarded on the ground is a sky blue cloth, symbolic of Heaven. Behind Lazarus are his sisters, Martha and Mary. Around stand the disciples and neighbours. The disciple holding the rope is Judas Iscariot, who betrayed Jesus. When Judas realised that his betrayal meant Jesus' death, he hanged himself. His prominence in this picture is a reminder of the close link in the Gospel between the raising of Lazarus and the death of Jesus. Jesus came back to Judaea to help Lazarus, giving his enemies their opportunity. All three of the stories of Jesus raising people from the dead point toward his own Resurrection, the central message of the gospel.

B. Elisha, in a deep blue cloak, raises his hand in prayer and blessing. On the ground lies the boy returning to life. Behind is the child's mother and a neighbour. In the Old Testament both Elijah and Elisha are described as raising a boy from the dead. These stories stress the power of God working through his prophets. One of the expectations of the coming of the Christ, or Messiah, was that the dead would be raised to

C

life. To his contemporaries, therefore, stories of Jesus raising people from the dead indicated that he was sent from God, like the Old Testament prophets. In Elisha's time the Israelites had no expectation of life after death, but by the time of Jesus most Jews believed that there would be a life-after-death for the righteous.

C. The principal figure is Jesus, riding a donkey, surrounded by disciples and pilgrims carrying palm branches. One disciple spreads a bright blue cloak. The man who has climbed a tree is probably Zacchaeus, though that happened earlier at Jericho. On the left a richly dressed man tells Jesus to reprimand his disciples, but Jesus points to the stones which, he said, would cry out if the disciples kept silent. The entry into Jerusalem is the one occasion in the Gospels when Jesus allowed his disciples to publicly call him by

Messianic titles such as 'Son of David'. This was a challenge to both religious and secular authorities. In the first century, Jews were expecting God to send a leader who would fight the Romans and claim back their land. By calling him 'Son of David' the crowd made known their belief that Jesus was that leader. In his temptations (see Window 7, scene C) Jesus had rejected military conquest, so he entered Jerusalem on a donkey instead of a horse. In modern terms, this is equivalent to using a car instead of a tank.

D. On the left is David carrying an enormous sword. Impaled on the point is the grotesque head of Goliath. The crowd welcoming the new hero includes a woman playing a harp, a man with a lute and women with pipes and a triangle. The dead tree on the skyline is balanced by the living tree in scene B, where Elisha brings the boy life. The giant Goliath was the champion of the Philistines, who lived in the five cities on the coast. Their attempt to conquer the whole land was thwarted by David. In the Old Testament, David is the founder of Judaea's ruling dynasty, so every succeeding king is a 'Son of David'. After they were conquered, Jews expressed their hope of deliverance as a longing for a 'Son of David'. Political and religious deliverance were spoken of in similar terms and shaded into each other.

The Chapel has only these two scenes from Jesus' ministry, similar to mediaeval books such as *Biblia Pauperum* and *Speculum Humanae Salvationis*, which also had little to say on the ministry. In the Christian calendar, the Triumphal Entry into Jerusalem is celebrated on the Sunday before Easter. Since mediaeval times it has been the custom to have processions and to bless and distribute palm crosses on Palm Sunday.

Window 9 *(left scenes)*

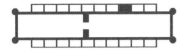

A. The Last Supper
St John 13:21–26
B. Bread in the wilderness
Exodus 16:14–35

DETAIL

All the stories about food in the Gospels point to the Last Supper and use the imagery of the manna in the wilderness, which is illustrated on the back cover of this guide.

A. Situated close to the altar, this scene depicts the origin of the central act of Christian worship, the Lord's Supper, or Eucharist (Thanksgiving). Jesus and all 12 disciples are shown sitting round a table. Jesus, on the left, under a red canopy, holds out the bread to Judas Iscariot, who leans forward to receive without touching,

A

just as the glazier would have received the consecrated bread at the Eucharist. Judas is clutching a money bag – his payment for betraying Jesus. Outside is the man with the water pot who had led them to the house. At the bottom of the picture is the jug and bowl with which Jesus had washed his disciples' feet, usually the task of a servant. This contrasts with the canopy, which, in Tudor society, marked the seat of a king.

B. In this scene, the manna wafers float down from the sky to be collected by the hungry Israelites. Most are using their hands, but one man has a winnowing tray, while a woman is catching them in her lap. Moses, carrying the Ten Commandments, and his brother Aaron stand on the left. Manna is a sweet substance produced when insects feed on tamarisk bushes and is found on the ground in the early morning. The Israelites saw its provision as an example of God's loving care, and in the Exodus story it is called 'bread' in the symbolic sense of food that sustains life. The link between this scene and the Last Supper goes back to the New Testament and includes the teaching after the feeding of the 5,000, when Jesus said, 'I am the Bread of Life' (John 6:35).

The disciples continued to break bread and bless wine in obedience to Jesus' command (for example, 1 Corinthians 11:23–26), so every Eucharist commemorates the Last Supper. Since the thirteenth century some Christians have especially celebrated this in the feast of Corpus Christi on the Thursday after Trinity Sunday.

Window 9 *(right scenes)*

C. Agony of Jesus in the garden
St Luke 22:39–46
D. Expulsion of the rebel angels
Revelation 12:7–9

These scenes have been contrasted to add meaning to each one. In the lower scene, Jesus resolves to obey his Father even if this brings suffering. Above, the rebellious angels disobey God. A detail of the Old Testament scene, showing the archangel Michael, is illustrated on the front cover of this guide.

C. The central figure is Jesus kneeling in prayer. On the rock is a cup that symbolises the suffering that awaits him. An angel flies down to support him in his obedience to his Father. Halos emphasise the sanctity of the occasion. In the foreground the three disciples, Peter, James and John, lie sleeping. They are wrapped in cloaks that have elaborate edges similar to copes, the most prestigious of all Church robes. In this way the glazier indicates the connection between the disciples and their successors, the bishops, abbots and deans of the early Church. Anti-clerical feeling was widespread in England, especially in London, in the early years of Henry VIII, before the Reformation. Many believed that the clergy, especially the senior ranks entitled to wear copes, were not sufficiently Christ-like to be worthy of the authority and privileges they claimed. Going to sleep when they should be praying would be seen as typical of their behaviour.

D. In the top left part of the picture, God Almighty sadly watches the expulsion of the rebel angels. Below him is the archangel Michael, in full late fifteenth-century Milanese armour, with a drawn sword. Other angels use poles to push the devils down into Hell, a place of fire and horror, filled with basilisks, legendary creatures shown here as black and indigo winged reptiles. In English

'Hell' refers to two separate concepts: Sheol, the waiting place of the dead (see Window 15, scene C), and Gehenna, the place of punishment. As in this window, Gehenna is typically depicted as a place of fire, brimstone and every possible horror. Many modern Christians believe Hell is exclusion from the presence of God, the logical result of ultimate and permanent rejection of him. Anything else negates God's gift of

free will. They see this as so dreadful that additional punishment would be irrelevant.

In the Middle Ages there was much speculation about the sin of the fallen angels. Pride, envy of mankind, love of their own excellence and desiring equality with God were all suggested. The emphasis here is on disobedience, in contrast to the obedience of Jesus.

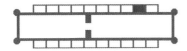

A. The betrayal of Jesus
St Matthew 26:47–56
B. Cain and Abel
Genesis 4:2–10

These scenes depict two betrayals by someone close. Judas Iscariot was one of the 12 chosen disciples, but he betrayed Jesus. Abel was murdered by his brother in a complete betrayal of family trust.

A. In the centre, Judas kisses Jesus to mark him out for arrest. Soldiers and officials gather round, one carrying a warrant. In the foreground, Peter raises his sword to strike Malchus, who is clutching his lantern, his name on his sleeve. The Gospels do not explain why Judas betrayed Jesus. He received 30 pieces of silver, but this was only the ritual price of a life (Exodus 21:32). Possibly he expected a different kind of saviour, such as a military conqueror, and was disillusioned.

B. The main picture shows Abel, in red on the ground, with Cain leaning over him, about to strike the final blow. Above, the two men are kneeling before the altar. On the left, smoke and flames from Abel's offering rise up toward Heaven. On the right, the smoke remains at ground level, as Cain's offering was not accepted, though Genesis does not explain why. His immediate resort to murder may indicate the answer.

The betrayal and arrest of Jesus took place in the Garden of Gethsemane, seen as parallel to the Garden of Eden, where Eve's disobedience led to expulsion from the garden (see Window 3, scene B). Paradise (from the Persian for 'garden') has come to mean Eternal Life, which is promised as a result of what happened in the Garden of Gethsemane.

Window 10 *(right scenes)*

C. The mocking of Jesus
St Luke 22:63–65
D. Shimei curses David
2 Samuel 16:5–13

DETAIL

Jesus is compared to King David because neither try to take revenge for insults and mocking. David did not always rise above the morality of his time, but on this occasion he did.

C. The central figure is Jesus, sitting on a chair in the palace of the High Priest, helpless, with his hands bound and his eyes blindfolded. Behind the chair a man raises his hand to strike. Priests and servants surround Jesus, making rude gestures as they call out insults and demand he uses his powers to say who hit him. Above is a gallery, from which the High Priest, Caiaphas, and his senior councillors watch the servants ill-treat the prisoner. The rude gestures seem pointless, as Jesus is blindfolded, but the glaziers 'translated' the verbal insults into visual ones for the silent visual medium of stained glass.
In the foreground is a dog, a symbol of fidelity or watchfulness. This incident took place during the night, a time for watchfulness, but the dog could also represent Jesus' fidelity to his Father's will.

D. The main figure is David, dressed in red with a blue cloak, in flight from Jerusalem to avoid capture by the army of his rebel son, Absolom. As he flees, Shimei, in blue on the left, curses and throws stones at him. David's escort, particularly his cousin Abishai, who is just behind David, want to kill Shimei for his insults. David restrains his cousin, saying that Shimei's attitude is understandable considering his own son, Absolom, had rebelled. David was weak when dealing with his family, but this scene shows him at his greatest and most Christ-like.

Christians see great significance in this New Testament scene, as they believe Jesus to be King of Kings with the power of judgement, yet he allowed himself to be badly treated in obedience to his Father's will. David also could have taken revenge but chose not to, which makes him a 'type' of Christ.

C

Window 11

A. The High Priest tries Jesus
St John 18:19–23
B. The imprisonment of Jeremiah
Jeremiah 37:11–16

C. The enquiry before Herod
St Luke 23:6–11
D. Noah's shame
Genesis 9:20–27

Jesus was rejected by both the religious and secular authorities of his nation. The scenes above show the comparable rejection of Jeremiah and the humiliating mocking of Noah.

A. On the left, Jesus is surrounded by soldiers and accusers. The High Priest is on the right. The base of his throne is inscribed, SIC RESPONDES PONTIFICUM ('Is that the way to answer the High Priest?' John 18:22). Pontiff had become a title of the Pope, and in the sixteenth century the authority of the Pope was hotly debated.

B. The Judean princes push Jeremiah into prison. Of all the Old Testament prophets, Jeremiah is seen as the most Christ-like. He spoke the truth as he saw it, was punished by the authorities, and he rejected the idea that God loved only one nation.

C. On the left is Herod Antipas, ruler of Galilee under the Romans. Jesus, on the right, seems remote from the scene as his accusers press charges. When Jesus did not produce a miracle, Herod's court mocked him.

D. Noah sprawls, drunk, on the ground, the mullion allowing discrete indication of his exposure. One son jeers at his father, but the other two act more respectfully. The Messenger's text is Isaiah 5:20, which refers to the loss of all sense of values, seen here and in Herod's dissolute court.

The contrasting sets of values portrayed in this window have a timeless resonance. Faithfulness to God, whatever the consequences, is set against the horrors of a society that has lost moral distinctions. 'Shame on you who call evil good and good evil', says the prophet.

Window 12

A. The scourging of Jesus
St John 19:1
B. The torments of Job
Job 2:7–10

C. Jesus is crowned with thorns
St John 19:2–3
D. The crowning of Solomon
Song of Songs 3:11

The scourging of Jesus is paralleled by a scene from the book of Job, the great Old Testament discussion about suffering. Jesus' crown of thorns is the ultimate irony for Christians, brought out by the contrasting Old Testament scene.

A. On the right, Jesus stands, stripped to his loincloth and tied to a red whipping post. To the left, a man in blue wields the fearsome 'flagrum' made of loaded leather thongs, the lower parts of which are already stained with blood. Above is Pilate, in red. His wife, her hand on his shoulder, pleads that Jesus is innocent, but to no avail.

B. The Old Testament book of Job begins with a strange folk tale of Job, who loses his wealth and suffers great pain but remains pious. The writer uses this story to explore the problem of suffering. In this scene, Job kneels on the left being beaten by demons, while his wife stands on the right urging him to curse God in his agony. Proverbially, 'Job's Comforters' are people who sympathise but cannot resist pointing out that the sufferer is at fault. Job's three friends gave him exactly that kind of comfort.

C. The seated figure is Jesus, still half naked, but with his robe thrown over his shoulders. On his head is a crown of thorns, pressed down with a stave. The crown of thorns was a piece of barrack-room humour by a group of Roman soldiers, who were amused that their prisoner claimed to be the King of the Jews.

D. On the left, Solomon is seated on a throne. On his right stands his mother, Bathsheba, holding a crown over her son's head. This imagery is unusual, as the emphasis in the Old Testament is usually on anointing

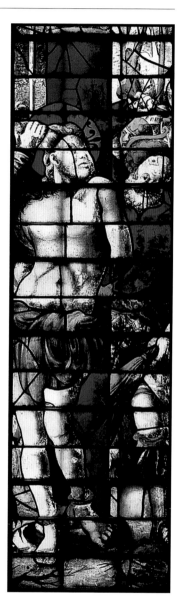

with oil. The crowning of Solomon by his mother had a deep significance for the Tudor dynasty as Margaret Beaufort had stood aside so her son, Henry VII, could take the throne. Unlike the figure in Window 4, Solomon does not look like Henry VIII; this window predates the development of that idea.

Jesus was human, so his physical suffering was real. The book of Job had earlier asked how suffering can be reconciled with belief in God. Christians hold that the suffering, Crucifixion and Resurrection of Jesus raise new questions but also show where answers may be found.

Window 13: East window

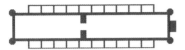

LOWER LEFT:
Ecce homo **(Behold the man)**
St John 19:5–7
LOWER MIDDLE:
Pilate washes his hands
St Matthew 27:24–25

The East Window is divided into six scenes from the New Testament, which tell the story of the death of Jesus. They should be viewed left to right, lower then upper. There are no Old Testament scenes. The first and second scenes indicate how Pilate, the Roman Governor, dealt with the accusations brought by the Jewish religious leaders.

LOWER LEFT: The central figure is Jesus, looking weary and resigned and still only wearing a loincloth, though his purple robe has been thrown over his shoulders. On his head is the crown of thorns. Jesus has been put forward by Pilate with the words 'Behold the man' (*Ecce homo*). The answer is a howled demand for Jesus' Crucifixion. The accusers are shown below; the one in a mitre on the right is clearly a religious leader. On the left of Jesus

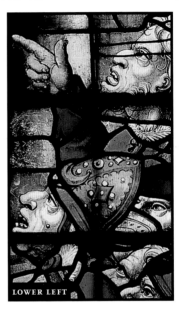

LOWER LEFT

stands Pilate, with Caiaphas beside him wearing a green cap.

LOWER MIDDLE: Pilate is in the centre, and Jesus is in front of him, his hands bound and the crown of thorns on his head. A servant holds a large copper dish and pours water over Pilate's hands. All four Gospels say that Pilate thought Jesus was innocent but, through fear of riots, was persuaded by the Jewish authorities to condemn him. Here, Pilate washes his hands of responsibility. Nonetheless, he gave authority for the execution.

In the Christian creed, the phrase 'Crucified under Pontius Pilate' is used mainly to date the event not blame Pilate alone. Pilate was responsible, but so were the Jewish religious authorities. The death of Jesus was brought about by factors common in human existence such as fear, selfishness and malice, so Christians accept that, in some sense, all are responsible.

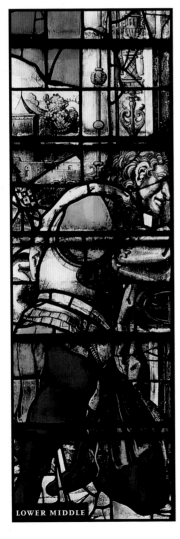

LOWER MIDDLE

LOWER RIGHT:
Jesus carries his Cross
St Luke 23:26–31
UPPER LEFT:
Jesus is nailed to the Cross
St Mark 15:24

The Via Dolorosa, or 'Way of the Cross', was the subject of pious devotion in the later Middle Ages. The Gospels mention briefly the way from Pilate's court to the place of execution, but there are legendary additions that make these scenes complex.

LOWER RIGHT: In the centre, Jesus carries the heavy, wooden, T-shaped Cross. The soldier on the right drags him along, while, on the left, Simon of Cyrene helps him. Veronica (lower left) has a cloth with which to wipe Jesus' face. Pilate and Caiaphas pass through the city gate in a chariot. On the right, the bright red patch of glass represents Aceldama, the field of Blood, which is connected to the death of Judas Iscariot, the disciple who had betrayed Jesus.

LOWER RIGHT

UPPER LEFT

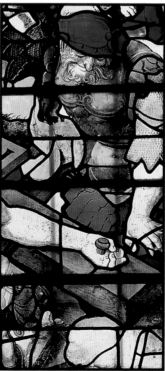

UPPER LEFT: Jesus stretched out on the Cross, which has been placed on the ground. A soldier hammers a nail into one hand, and another collects his tools. Pilate and Caiaphas watch from their chariot. Crucifixion was a deliberately brutal form of public torture that was used as a deterrent. Roman citizens were exempt from crucifixion: it was reserved for rebels, escaped slaves and bandits. In these windows Jesus is shown nailed to the Cross, whereas the thieves are tied. Different methods could have been used, but the soldiers are unlikely to have differentiated in this way on one occasion.

The Crucifixion of Jesus is remembered on the Friday before Easter – Good or Holy Friday. Christians have used the cross as their main symbol since the early fourth century. A crucifix, that is a cross with a figure, stresses the suffering of Jesus, while an empty cross also commemorates his Resurrection.

UPPER MIDDLE

UPPER RIGHT:
The descent from the Cross
St John 19:38–40

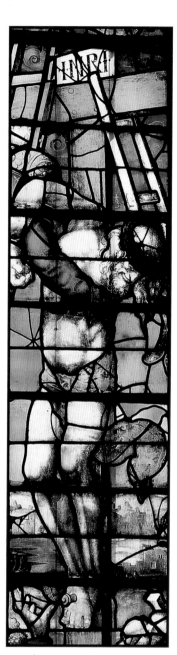

These scenes show the Crucifixion of Jesus, the defining moment of Christianity. INRI (on the Cross) are the first letters, in Latin, of the title 'Jesus of Nazareth, King of the Jews'. Jesus was put to death because he claimed to be the Messiah, or Christ.

UPPER MIDDLE: The figure on the central Cross is Jesus, still wearing the crown of thorns. On the right is the thief who repented, and on the left is the more contorted body of the other thief. At the base of the Cross the soldiers dice while they wait. On the left, a soldier is about to pierce the side of Jesus to check that he is dead. Mary the Mother of Jesus, the disciple John, whom Jesus had asked to look after her, and Mary of Magdala stand on the right. The centurion who said 'truly this was the Son of God', when he saw how Jesus died, is in the background, with his words on a scroll above his head (*Vere filius dei erat iste*). Above, the sun and moon symbolise the sorrow of all creation at the death of Jesus. The 'instruments of the passion' of traditional devotion include the hammer and nails, the crown of thorns, the lance, the dice and the INRI superscription.

UPPER RIGHT: Crucifixion usually took several days, but there was need for haste, as it was the eve of the Sabbath. The legs of the thieves were broken to speed up their death, but Jesus had already died. This scene shows men on ladders, lifting the body of Jesus down from the Cross. On the left is Joseph of Arimathaea, and on the right is the centurion who said Jesus was innocent. At the foot of the Cross, Nicodemus is reaching up to drag out a nail. In the foreground, Mary, the Mother of Jesus, in a state of collapse, is supported by John the disciple and Mary of Magdala. According to the Gospels, Joseph of

Arimathaea was, like Nicodemus, a member of the Jewish Council, so he was able to approach Pilate to gain permission to bury the body of Jesus. In other parts of the Roman Empire the bodies of criminals were left on crosses as a deterrent. Because of Jewish objections to this practice, in Palestine the Roman authorities allowed them to be buried, usually in the common grave. Joseph's intervention prevented the body of Jesus from being buried in this way.

The five wounds of Christ referred to in popular devotions are the four nail holes in his hands and feet and the lance wound in his side. The five crosses embroidered on altar cloths represent these wounds. Some people who have meditated on the wounds of Christ are believed to have received the stigmata, or marks, in the same five places. The best known is Francis of Assisi.

Window 14

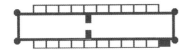

A. Naomi mourns for her son
Ruth 1:5–6
B. The brazen serpent
Numbers 21:8–9

C. Mourning for Jesus
Early Christian legend
D. The brazen serpent
Numbers 21:8–9

Superficially this window concentrates on death, but deeper consideration shows the emphasis on life: Ruth reminds us of the glorious days of David; and the death of Jesus precedes his Resurrection.

C. The body of Jesus is held by his weeping mother, while Joseph of Arimathaea kneels by the head. Gathered round the central figures are two of the women with John and Nicodemus (or, possibly, the centurion). On the ground are the nails, bowl and sponge. In the Renaissance, great stress was put on the stages of mourning for Jesus, though the Gospels indicate that his burial was hurried because the Sabbath was immanent.

A. The three mourning women are Naomi and her daughters-in-law, Ruth and Orpath. The death of Naomi's son had made all three childless widows, without support, so she returned to her kin in Judah. Ruth, declaring her belief in the God of Israel, chose to go with her, and there she became the ancestress of King David. This scene, like the one beside it, depicts the grief that precedes the glory.

B and D. Unique in the Chapel, the upper five lights present one picture. Originally there was only the upper window, but in the 1840s the lower part was opened up. Scenes A and C were moved down, and the designer, J. H. Hedgeland, ignored the pattern in the other windows so his picture could fit comfortably across the five lights. It is based on Rubens' painting *The Brazen Serpent* (National Gallery, London). On the left Moses lifts the wooden Cross bearing the serpent, while his brother, Aaron, encourages the stricken Israelites to look at it. The dying people on the right have vicious snakes writhing round them. This choice of picture fits the typological pattern of the Chapel. It is one of the 'types' of the Crucifixion found in the thirteenth-century book *Biblia Pauperum*. The idea, however, goes back to the New Testament, in which John 3:14 says the Son of Man will be lifted up just as the serpent was lifted up in the wilderness, thereby bringing Eternal Life.

The Lamentation for Jesus is hardly marked in the liturgy of Western Christianity but the Good Friday evening Epitaphion procession of the Dead Christ, with its flower covered bier, is an important ceremony in the Eastern Orthodox Church.

Window 15

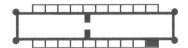

A. The burial of Jesus
St Matthew 27:57–61
B. Joseph is thrown into the pit
Genesis 37:18–24

C. The harrowing of hell
1 Peter 3:19–20
D. The Exodus
Exodus 14:21–30

Despair turning to joy is the theme of this window. On the left is the burial of Jesus and the attempted murder of Joseph. On the right is the harrowing, or breaking up, of Hell and the Israelites' release from slavery.

A. The body of Jesus is lowered into the tomb by Joseph of Arimathaea and Nicodemus. His mother, Mary, is supported by John and one of the women, while Mary of Magdala places the crown of thorns in front. The tomb is shown as a Renaissance sarcophagus instead of the stone ledges in a cave that would have been used in first-century Palestine.

B. Joseph is pushed into the pit by his brothers. Above, his cloak is soaked in blood to convince his father of his death. When Joseph disappeared from the pit (see Window 17) he apparently died, only to reappear in the glory of high office in Egypt, saving his family from death during a famine. This 'death', 'resurrection' and 'salvation' were seen as similar to those of Jesus.

C. Christ, with the nail marks clearly visible, helps Adam ('Everyman') out of the dungeon of Hell. The door is broken, and the devils cower away. One English word, 'Hell', has to cover two ideas: Gehenna, the state of damnation (see Window 9, scene D), and Sheol, the waiting place of the dead. This is Sheol, from which Jesus released the righteous who had died, to be with him in Heaven. There is a brief reference in the New Testament, but later traditions elaborated on this idea.

D. In the centre Moses, in blue, holds his staff high, leading the Israelites up from the Red Sea after their release from slavery in Egypt. In the middle distance the chariots

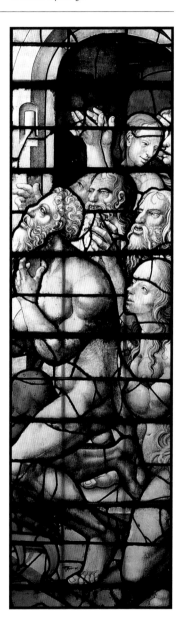

of the pursuing army flounder. The Exodus is the most important incident in the Old Testament and holds the same central position as the death and Resurrection of Jesus does in the New. In both, all hope seemed dead, but God brought salvation.

Jesus is buried in a garden, referring back to the Garden of Eden, where disobedience meant expulsion and death. Now, the obedience of Jesus means that Hell is harrowed and the dead, forgiven and sanctified, rise to glory in Paradise (Persian for 'garden').

Window 16

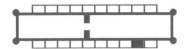

A. The Resurrection of Jesus
St Matthew 28:2–4
B. Jonah and the sea monster
Jonah 2:10

C. Jesus appears to his mother
Early Christian legend
D. Tobias returns home
Tobit 11:6–9

This window depicts the Resurrection of Jesus, the central and defining belief of Christianity. The Gospels indicate that he rose from the dead early in the morning on the third day after his Crucifixion.

A. The central figure is that of Jesus rising from his tomb, shown as a sixteenth-century sarcophagus with the lid half off, rather than a first-century Palestinian cave with the stone door rolled away. The soldiers on guard are staggering back, but Jesus' hand is raised in blessing. The nail marks are on his hands and feet, and the javelin wound is just above his heart.

B. On the left, Jonah steadies himself as he climbs out of the sea monster's mouth. The monster has been foreshortened so its mouth and great eye are prominent and the coils of its body lie behind. This story is used as a 'type' of the Resurrection in the New Testament; Jonah's three days in the monster's belly are compared with the time Jesus spent in the tomb. An ancient Middle Eastern myth described how the Deity conquered Chaos in the shape of a sea monster and so ordered the world. The Bible uses this imagery, especially in poetic passages, to praise God for keeping in check the forces of evil and chaos. Jesus' conquest of death comes into the same category. The old translation, 'whale', does not convey adequately the mythological and biblical symbolism of the story.

C. Jesus, carrying a victory banner, greets his mother, Mary, who had been praying for comfort on his death. There is no New Testament account of this appearance, but Ambrose, the fourth-century Bishop of Milan, was one of many who was sure Jesus would have appeared to her first.

D. Anna had given her son up for lost but is here shown greeting him and his companion, the angel Raphael in disguise. Tobias' faithful dog is in the foreground. Mediaeval scholars saw this story of a mother's grief for her lost son as a parallel to the grief of Mary. Like Mary, Anna's grief ends in joy when her son returns.

In the Resurrection death did its worst, but Jesus was victorious. The message in the right-hand lights is that resurrection includes knowing and being known to those whom we love, as it is more than a formless continuance.

Window 17 *(left scenes)*

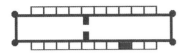

A. The women come to the tomb
St Mark 16:1–2
B. Reuben finds the pit empty
Genesis 37:29–30

The left-hand lights of this window illustrate the mystery of the empty tomb. Early on the Sunday morning, the women came and found the tomb empty, without explanation. The Old Testament 'type' is from the story of Joseph.

A. According to the Gospels, Jesus had been hastily buried on the Friday evening by Joseph of Arimathea. The haste was because of the immanence of the Sabbath, during which no work could be done and the city gates were closed. So, as soon as they could, at dawn on the Sunday, the women came to the tomb bringing perfumed oils with which to anoint the body of Jesus as their last service to him. Here they are shown not knowing what to do, as the body has gone. Their leader, Mary of Magdala, in red on the left, has put her jar on the ground. The Gospels refer to a number of women coming to the tomb. Tradition in religious art has settled on three: Mary of Magdala, Mary Cleopas and Mary Salome. Mary Cleopas was the wife of Cleopas, one of the disciples who walked to Emmaus (see Window 18, scene A). Mary Salome may have been the wife of Zebedee and mother of James and John, disciples of Jesus.

B. This scene is the sequel to scene B in Window 15, which shows Joseph being pushed into the pit. Here Reuben is shown gazing down into the pit, looking for his brother. He had intended to rescue Joseph but found he had disappeared. In the background, two more brothers are looking after the sheep. Joseph was taken into Egypt by passing merchants, sold as a slave and rose to high office so was able to help his family during a famine. Joseph is seen as a 'type' of Jesus because his suffering and apparent death resulted in salvation for his people. In the window Reuben's despair at the disappearance and presumed death of his brother is paralleled wtih the despair of the women at the death of Jesus and the disappearance of his body.

Little is said in the Gospels about the empty tomb because the apostles preached the 'good news' (or gospel) that Jesus had risen from the dead, which was their explanation for the empty tomb. The authorities gave their own explanation when they accused the disciples of stealing the body, and this is countered in Matthew's Gospel with the story of the setting of the guard (see Window 16, scene A).

Window 17 *(right scenes)*

C. Jesus appears to Mary of Magdala
St John 20:11–17
D. Daniel in the lion's den
Daniel 6:10–22

DETAIL

These scenes continue the theme of the Resurrection of Jesus, depicting his meeting with Mary of Magdala on the Sunday morning. Daniel in the lion's den, parallels the Resurrection but is not specific to Mary's meeting.

C. Jesus is shown dressed as a gardener, holding a long, narrow, fenland spade and with a broad hat pushed off the back of his head. The mark of a nail can be seen on one of his hands. On the right, Mary kneels, wanting to touch him to convince herself that it is really Jesus. She had mistaken him for the gardener, and it was not until he spoke that she recognised him. This scene is often called *Noli me tangere* (Latin for 'touch me not'), a translation of Jesus' words. It was not appropriate for her to clutch at him, as resurrection is not just a renewal of life but a different type of existence. Jesus sent Mary to tell the disciples that he had risen from the dead. Mary of Magdala therefore became the 'Apostle to the Apostles', which has been used by some to argue that the ministry of women has been wrongly restricted.

D. On the left, Daniel kneels in prayer surrounded by the lions. On the right stands King Darius, hardly able to believe that Daniel has survived. Above are earlier parts of the story – Daniel praying and being arrested. When Daniel was thrown into the lion's den, everyone gave him up for dead. When he was found alive and untouched by the lions, his survival was a kind of resurrection, which is why the mediaeval scholars used it in this way. Mediaeval 'Bestiaries' said that a lion cub was born dead and remained so for three days, then its father breathed on it and it came to life. This 'natural history' explains why lions symbolise Jesus' Resurrection.

The Resurrection is such an important part of Christian belief and theology that it is not surprising so many windows in the Chapel are devoted to it. The story of Mary's meeting is often read at Easter Sunday morning services. She is commemorated on 22 July.

C

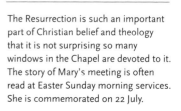

Window 18

A. On the road to Emmaus
St Luke 24:13–27
B. Tobias meets the angel
Tobit 5:4–8

C. The supper at Emmaus
St Luke 24:28–30
D. Daniel fed by the prophet
Daniel 14:33–39

The stranger on the road, who is more than he first appears, links the left-hand scenes. The life-giving importance of food, both physical and spiritual, connects the right-hand scenes. Both themes have implications for Christian discipleship.

A. On the first Easter day, two disciples walking to their village are joined by a stranger. When they describe their despair and disappointment at the death of Jesus, he explains the teaching of the Old Testament prophets that salvation comes through the suffering of the Messiah: for example, in Isaiah 53, which is called 'the song of the suffering servant.' The stranger is on the left of the window, with a wide-brimmed traveller's hat. A significant nail mark is visible on his right hand. The road is noticeably stony, reflecting the disciples' bewilderment.

B. On the left is Tobias, and on the right is the archangel Raphael disguised as the young man Azarius, though his red and green wings are visible. Azarius offers to accompany Tobias on his journey. This is the first of several scenes from the adventures of Tobias in the Chapel (see also, in the order of the story, windows 2, 16 and 24). Raphael accompanies him throughout as guide and protector.

C. On the left, Jesus is seated at the table. The disciples, one seated opposite and the other standing, realised who Jesus was as he broke the bread. On the table is the bread, tumblers and a jug of wine. Many of the New Testament accounts of the Resurrection appearances involve food, which points to the continuing meeting with Jesus in the bread and wine of Christian worship.

D. On the right Daniel prays in the lions' den. Top left, the prophet Habakkuk, carrying a basket of food, flies to his aid, supported by an angel, who has a hand in his hair. Hezekiah had been taking food to the reapers in the Judaean fields when the angel whisked him to Babylon as Daniel, in the lion's den for seven days, was in danger of starving. This strange story is found in the Apocrypha.

The earliest name for Christianity was 'the Way' – a way of life, following the teaching of Jesus. The metaphor of Christian discipleship as a journey is still used, and the story of the walk to Emmaus is a reminder of the promise of the continuing fellowship of Jesus.

Window 19

A. Jesus appears to Thomas
St John 20:24–29
B. The return of the prodigal son
St Luke 15:20–24

C. Jesus appears to the apostles
St John 20:19–20
D. Joseph greets his father
Genesis 46:29–30

The general theme in this window is rejoicing at an unexpected return. Instead of an Old Testament incident, the upper left scene is of a parable of Jesus. The lower scenes have been exchanged, as the right should preceed the left.

A. Thomas was not with the disciples when Jesus appeared (see scene C) so expressed doubts, which were answered by this appearance. Jesus stands on the right with his hand guiding Thomas', but, seeing Jesus, Thomas is unwilling to touch in the way he had demanded before.

B. On the left, the father embraces his son, who kneels asking forgiveness, his rags in sharp contrast to the rich robes of everyone else. Servants bring out rich clothes, and and a feast is prepared. The emphasis is on the lavishness of the welcome.

C. On the right Jesus, in red, holding a triumphal banner, raises a hand in blessing, the nail marks very visible. The apostles show their surprise and shock at his unexpected appearance. The doors behind are firmly shut for fear of the authorities.

D. In the centre, Jacob embraces his son Joseph whom he had thought dead. Joseph's 11 brothers look on in some trepidation in case he wants revenge. Joseph's gold chain and the extensive palace in the background indicate the high office to which he has risen.

All these scenes show the reaction to a completely unexpected return from death or apparent death. The Gospel writers make it very clear that the Resurrection of Jesus was unexpected. Thomas is the one called 'The Doubter', but he was not the only one to doubt.

Window 20 *(left scenes)*

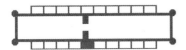

A. The Ascension of Jesus
Acts of the Apostles 1:9
B. Elijah is carried up to Heaven
2 Kings 2:11–13

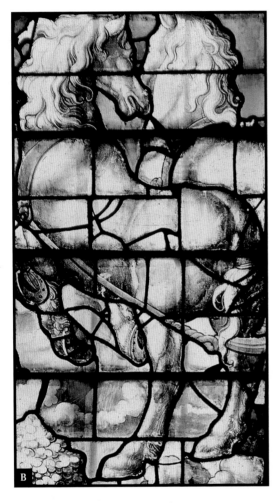

The Resurrection appearances of Jesus end with his Ascension into Heaven, which is depicted in the left-hand lights of this window. The upper scene is of the ascension of Elijah, one of the most outstanding prophets of the Old Testament.

A. The disciples stand round a mound, from which Jesus has ascended, gazing into the sky. In the top left of the picture, the feet and part of the robe of Jesus can be seen

disappearing into the cloud. This incident is a kind of 'acted parable', in which Jesus clearly brings to an end the period in which he appeared to his disciples. His presence with them will be experienced differently from this time forward.

B. The chariot of fire carrying Elijah up to Heaven is in the upper part of the window, and below is Elisha reaching up. Elijah leans out of the chariot to throw down his cloak to his disciple, threby nominating Elisha as his successor. In the Bible fire often symbolises the presence of God.

Belief in life after death was not part of Israelite religion in Elijah's time, so this story stresses how exceptional he was seen to be.

In the Christian calendar, the Ascension of Jesus is celebrated 40 days after Easter. To a Christian, Heaven is a different type of existence, in which the four dimensions (three of space and one of time) are irrelevant. However, the symbolism of Heaven being 'up there' continues to be used for convenience.

Window 20 *(right scenes)*

C. The Holy Spirit descends on the apostles
Acts of the Apostles 2:1–4
D. Moses receives the Law
Exodus 31:18

DETAIL

The coming of the Holy Spirit at Pentecost is seen as the birth of the Christian Church. In the same way, the giving of the law to Moses set the people of Israel on their unique course.

C. The lower scene is dominated by the dove, surrounded by an aureole, which is a field of light and radiance symbolising divinity. Below, the apostles are seated in a room with, in the middle, Mary the mother of Jesus. Flames from the aureole reach down to the heads of those gathered below. The account in Acts refers to a

mighty rushing wind and tongues of flame. Fire and wind are often associated in the Bible with the presence of God and, together with the dove, are used as symbols of the Holy Spirit. The Holy Spirit is the aspect of God that is present with the believer, and indicates that God is immanent (close) as well as transcendent (beyond and above).

D. High in the upper lights, Moses reaches out to grasp the stone tablets of the Law from God, whose figure is surrounded by an aureole. Protruding from Moses' head are the small horns usual in pictures of Moses at Sinai (see comment on Window 6, scene B). Below, the Israelites wait for his return. Directly opposite, Window 6 tells the next part of the story, in which they tire of waiting and build a Golden Calf to worship, angering Moses as he came down the mountain. The Jewish religious calendar commemorated this giving of the Law 50 days after Pesach (Passover); in the New Testament this Jewish festival is called Pentecost.

Peter and the other disciples began to proclaim the good news (gospel) of the resurrection of Jesus in the open streets and public places of Jerusalem, to the consternation of the authorities. Those who had followed Jesus received the news of his Resurrection gladly and were baptised into the 'Fellowship of the Way' (the earliest name for Christianity. From Jerusalem it was taken to Rome, Edessa, Spain, India and 'the ends of the earth'.

Window 21

A. Peter preaches in the Temple
Acts of the Apostles 2:14
B. Peter heals the lame man
Acts of the Apostles 3:1–11

C. The death of Ananias
Acts of the Apostles 5:1–11
D. The apostles under arrest
Acts of the Apostles 5:40–41

These four scenes are all stories of Peter from the Acts of the Apostles. It was unusual to include such scenes, but Bishop Fox, who drew up the window plan, was a scholar of the New Learning so had studied Acts.

A. Peter leads a group of the apostles into the Temple, shown as a great Renaissance cathedral complete with a statue of Moses carrying the stone tablets of the Law. In the middle distance Peter preaches from a pulpit. The Temple in Jerusalem was a very different kind of place. It had comparatively small buildings, was dominated by great courtyards, and would have had no statues of any kind. It had been magnificently rebuilt by Herod the Great but was destroyed in 70AD and only the 'Wailing Wall' now remains.

B. On the left, the lame man sits begging from those coming through the Golden Gate. His leg is at a very odd angle, and his crutch is on the ground by his side. On the right, Peter, with John behind him, tells him to rise in the name of Jesus. The arch behind represents the Golden Gate of the Temple, which was the entrance on the eastern side from the Kidron valley and the Mount of Olives.

C. In the foreground, Ananias collapses, probably from the shock of being revealed as a liar. Behind, Peter stands with the other apostles who indicate their concern at what has happened. Ananias had attempted to make out that he was far more generous than he was actually prepared to be. In the sixteenth century people were increasingly critical of this type of hypocrisy in their contemporaries.

D. In the centre, Peter, surrounded by soldiers, is led from the Temple with the other apostles. In the middle distance is a small picture of them being beaten. Acts describes a short period when the apostles' preaching about the Resurrection of Jesus was tolerated in Jerusalem, but this soon came to an end as the Authorities attempted to stop them by arrests, beatings, imprisonment and execution.

This window makes clear Peter's position as the leader of the early Church as indicated in the Acts of the Apostles. To what extent Peter's position had been inherited by the Pope was a matter of debate and division at the time the window was painted.

Window 22

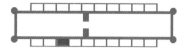

A. Paul and Barnabas at Lystra
Acts of the Apostles 14:8–13
B. The conversion of Paul
Acts of the Apostles 9:3–7

C. Paul stoned
Acts of the Apostles 14:19
D. Paul escapes from Damascus
Acts of the Apostles 9:19

This window, like its two neighbours, has four scenes from the Acts of the Apostles with no Old Testament 'types'. They should be considered in the order B, D, A, C. They describe the conversion of Paul, his early preaching and its effects.

B. In the foreground, Paul, who has fallen from his horse, raises his arm to protect his eyes from the bright light that strikes down from the sky. In the background, the soldiers accompanying him scatter in all directions. Paul had been a witness and approver of the stoning to death of Stephen in Jerusalem and had led a persecution of the Christians. He had been sent by the High Priest to do the same in Damascus but had a dramatic encounter on the road, seeing a bright light and hearing a voice which he identified as Jesus. He became a follower of Jesus and was as enthusiastic in preaching about him as he had previously been in persecuting Christians.

D. In the centre, Paul holds a book in his left hand as he preaches, raising his right hand to enforce his argument. In the foreground, a man studies the Scriptures to verify what has been said. Paul went further than Peter and the other apostles in stressing that Jesus had made the Law of Moses redundant. He caused great anger by his preaching, particularly among those who had accompanied him from Jerusalem, expecting him to lead a persecution of the Christians. He had to be smuggled out of Damascus for his own safety. In the background, on the left, is the laundry basket in which he escaped, being lowered down the wall by the Damascan Christians.

M 2

A. On the left, Paul recoils when the priest of Jupiter in Lystra prepares to sacrifice an ox to him. Barnabas stands, equally horrified, behind him. The priest holds a garland for the ceremony. A local legend meant that the people were expecting Jupiter and Mercury to appear in human form and thought the arrival of Paul and Barnabas fulfilled this expectation. Lystra was in the upland area of modern Turkey, and, as well as preaching to the Jews, Paul spoke

about Jesus to non-Jews, especially those who attended the synagogues. He believed he was called to spread the gospel among non-Jews in the Roman Empire.

C. On the left Paul moves away, while a soldier picks up a rock to throw. The people of Lystra had greeted the apostles with such enthusiasm that they suggested sacrificing to them, but when Paul and Barnabas rejected the sacrifice the mood turned ugly. Most of the people of Lystra were worshippers of the local version of the Classical religion of Jupiter, Mercury and the other Greek and Roman deities. When Paul visited a place he first preached to the Jews and to those non-Jews who attended synagogue. The latter often proved especially interested in the message of Christianity, and they were the way by which Christianity spread to the general population.

M2. This messenger is dressed as a sixteenth-century scholar with a doctor's cap and robe. It is suggested that the painter intended to remind people of Erasmus and his stay in Cambridge 25 years before. The ox at the knee of the messenger identifies him as Luke, who wrote Acts of the Apostles, from which the scenes in this window are taken. In religious art the ox has been assigned to Luke because of his emphasis on the sacrificial aspects of Jesus' ministry. The painter used the same design but with different colours for M1 in this window and M1 and M3 in Window 21.

Paul was the most significant thinker in the early Church, and his conversion and preaching changed Christianity from an internal reform movement within Judaism to the worldwide faith of today. Paul's conversion is commemorated on 25 January.

Window 23

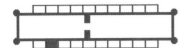

A. Paul says farewell
Acts of the Apostles 20:38
B. Paul heals the possessed girl
Acts of the Apostles 16:17–18

C. Paul before the Emperor Nero
Early Christian legend
D. Paul tried by the Governor
Acts of the Apostles 25:6–12

This window, like 21 and 22, has four scenes about the early Church. They describe the latter part of the ministry of Paul and should be taken in the order B, A, D, C.

B. On the right, Paul gestures toward the girl who is on the left with her owners beside her. When she was healed, she could no longer earn money for them from divination, so they had Paul arrested. This is shown above the main scene on the left. Jesus healed possessed people and gave authority to his followers to do the same. An important factor was always the belief of the sufferer that the healer had that authority.

A. Paul, on the left, says farewell to a group of believers. He believed he was called to establish churches in new areas so moved on frequently. This scene must have been repeated many times. The ship on which he is

to travel is shown, above, at anchor. A small boat, carrying a passenger, is being rowed out to it. It is depicted as a Tudor ship, such as those that Henry VIII used in the 1520s when he visited France.

D. Paul, on the right, stands before Festus, the new Governor of Palestine, who is sitting on an elaborate judgement seat. Paul's accusers stand around, jeering and shouting accusations. He had been arrested in the Temple in Jerusalem then taken to Caesarea, where he was in prison for two years. This hearing ends with Paul taking advantage of his Roman citizenship and making an Appeal to Caesar.

C. The Emperor Nero, wearing an imperial crown, stands on the right. On the left, Paul is brought forward by the soldier who had escorted him from Palestine after his Appeal. Acts of the Apostles does not describe any trial in Rome, so this comes from an early legend. Nero's drawn sword indicates how Paul was executed.

After the fire that destroyed much of Rome in 64, people started to blame Nero for the catastrophe. He began a persecution of the Christians to divert attention from himself. Both Peter and Paul are believed to have died in this persecution. In the Christian calendar they are commemorated on 29 June.

Window 24

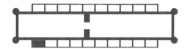

A. The death of Mary
Early Christian legend
B. The death of Tobit
Tobit 14:3–11

C. The funeral of Mary
Early Christian legend
D. The funeral of Jacob
Genesis 50:12–14

This window depicts the death and burial of Mary. She is shown clearly as being at the centre of the early Church. The window has suffered considerable damage over the centuries, and therefore the scenes are not very clear.

A. The apostles reunite round the deathbed of Mary. John, in red on the right, supports her hand, which is holding a candle. Peter stands on the left, and the others gather round. In Acts 1:14 Mary is mentioned as being with the apostles, but there is no subsequent reference to her in the New Testament. John's Gospel says that Jesus, while on the Cross, asked John to look after her, so in all paintings, including this one, John is shown as closely supportive of Mary. Some traditions suggest she went to live with him in Ephesus when he led the Church there.

B. Tobit lies on the right with his head propped on a pillow. His son, Tobias, and the angel Raphael face him. His wife, Anna, and daughter-in-law, Sarah, are on either side. This is the fourth scene from the book of Tobit to be found in the Chapel (see in story order windows 18, 2 and 16). The book was written toward the end of the third century BC but not included in the Scriptures by the Jewish Rabbis. It was popular among Greek-speaking Jews of the Dispersion, so became part of the Christian Old Testament. During the Reformation period, Protestants started to use the Jewish Old Testament. Books like Tobit were put aside in the Apocrypha.

C. According to legend, Mary's funeral was attacked by an armed band, but one of the attackers found that his hands, which had seized the bier to tip it over, were miraculously struck off and stuck to the pall. The

hands can be seen stuck to the pall in the centre, and the armed band can be picked out above the main picture on the left. The repetition of these legends shows the importance of Mary to mediaeval Christians. English people, including Henry VIII, went in pilgrimage to her shrine at Walsingham in Norfolk, where a Saxon woman had obeyed a vision and built a replica of Mary's home in Nazareth.

D. On the right, Jacob's bier is carried by five of his sons out of the gate of the city. In the foreground, Joseph, in a rich robe and turban, stands ready to follow the funeral. On the left are other mourners also preparing to follow the bier. Jacob had died in

Egypt, but his sons took him back to Palestine to bury him in the family grave in the cave Abraham had bought in Hebron. There are several scenes from the story of Joseph in the Chapel (see windows 15, 17 and 19) as his story, though not his character, made him a 'type' of Christ.

In spite of the extensive damage, there is no evidence to suggest that this window attracted the iconoclasts more than others in the Chapel. However, the subject of this window would have particularly annoyed sixteenth- and seventeenth-century Protestants as they felt that adoration of Mary detracted from the worship more correctly given to her son.

Window 25

A. The assumption of Mary
Early Christian legend
B. Enoch is taken up to Heaven
Genesis 5:24

C. The coronation of Mary
Early Christian legend
D. Solomon crowns his mother
1 Kings 2:19

This window concludes the legends of Mary that began with her miraculous birth in the windows opposite. The 'types' are from the Old Testament, and the reason why they were chosen is straightforward correspondence with the New Testament scenes below.

A. Mary's hands are together in prayer, and she is standing on a downward pointing sickle moon that represents the transitory nature of the world she is leaving. Two angels are carrying the moon with its burden up toward Heaven, while another two support Mary's shoulders. Others play musical instruments, including a lute and a harp. Mary is in blue because this is the colour of Heaven and heavenly love.

B. Enoch is carried up to Heaven by angels. The cryptic reference in Genesis is 'God had taken him away'. From this it was assumed that, because of his perfect fellowship with God, he was taken to Heaven without dying (for example, in the letter to the Hebrews 11:5). In *Biblia Pauperum*, a thirteenth-century book that is full of the typology of the period, Enoch's story is used as a 'type' for the Ascension of Jesus, but it is equally suitable here.

C. Mary is crowned by Christ while, on the right, the Father looks on. Above, the dove of the Holy Spirit completes the Trinity. In the later Middle Ages it was usual for all three figures of the Trinity to be represented, not a sole figure, as earlier. Below the main figures are four angels – the one on the left is playing a dulcimer (see detail), and another is looking at music, while the two on the right are playing shawms. Above the main figures are more angels singing.

D. It is not certain whether these figures represent Solomon and Bathsheba or Esther and Ahasuerus. Both are regular 'types' of the Coronation of Mary, but the scrolls of the top two Messengers are blank. Solomon and Bathsheba are already in the Chapel (Window 12), which suggests the other pair, but an inscription on a medallion in the canopy refers to the King of Israel, so Solomon is more likely. The Solomon story was particularly important for the Tudors because of the relationship of Margaret of Beaufort with her son, Henry VII.

Those Christians who celebrate the Assumption of Mary do so on 15 August. The important aspect of this story is that Mary's body was reunited with her soul in unique anticipation of the Resurrection.